Know About
Mahabharata

Know about Mahabharata

ALL RIGHTS RESERVED. No part of this book may be reproduced in a retrieval system or transmitted in any form or by any means electronics, mechanical, photocopying, recording and or without permission of the publisher.

Published by

MAPLE PRESS PRIVATE LIMITED
office: A-63, Sector 58, Noida 201301, U.P., India
phone: +91 120 455 3581, 455 3583
email: info@maplepress.co.in
website: www.maplepress.co.in

Reprinted in 2019

ISBN: 978-93-50335-63-5

Contents

Preface 5
1. Story of King Shantanu 6
2. The Kingdom of Hastinapur 10
3. Story of Arjuna 13
4. Story of Eklavya 17
5. Karna 21
6. Envious Duryodhana 25
7. Pandavas Stay in the Forest 29
8. Marriage of Pandavas 31
9. Indraprastha 35
10. Game of Dice 39
11. Second Game of Dice 43
12. Life in Exile 46
13. Story of Sage Durvasa 49
14. Skilful Arjuna 52
15. Disguise 55
16. Story of Keechaka 58
17. War Clouds Loom Large 60
18. War of Kurukshetra 63
19. Krishna Preached Gita 66
20. Downfall of Bhishma 69
21. Dronacharya Takes Over 72
22. Story Comes to an End 76

Preface

The Indian epic - *The Mahabharata* - is said to be the greatest epic of all times. With the addition of thousands of philosophies and lessons, the epic came to its present length. 'Maha' means greatness and 'Bharata' means triumph or victory. *The Mahabharata* is the longest epic poem in any language, constituting some 8800 verses in its original form composed by Vyasa and known as the "Jaya" (or "Victory"). The final version of *Mahabharata* as recited by Ugrasrava Sauti contains more than 100,000 verses. The main theme of the epic is the rivalry between the cousins, the Pandavas and the Kauravas, over the rulership of the kingdom of Hastinapur, which reaches its climactic point with the great battle of Kurukshetra. *The Mahabharata* is the largest epic in the history of mankind surpassing *The Ramayana* by Valmiki and *The Iliad* and *The Odyssey* by Homer. In accordance with the Indian tradition, *The Mahabharata* is sometimes referred to as the Fifth Veda.

CHAPTER 1
Story of King Shantanu

The kingdom of the Kuru king, Shantanu prospered around Hastinapur. Business and commerce, peace and prosperity, art and literature flourished all around. People, both inside the palace and outside, were happy.

Once King Shantanu went for hunting and decided to return to his palace in a ferryboat. The boatman, fisherman by caste, recognised the king. He requested the king to accept his hospitality in his humble hut.

The king agreed. The boatman offered all the delicacies that he could afford. He called his daughter to serve the honoured guest. And, as fate had it, the king fell in love with the fisherman's daughter (Satyavati) at first sight. Thereafter, the king started making secret visits to the fisherman's house in order to woo Satyavati and make her fall in love with him.

King Shantanu had already been a part of a short-lived marriage with the river Goddess-Ganga. Ganga had borne him a son who was named Devavratha. He was the most powerful, intelligent and glorious of all the Kurus.

His truthfulness, bravery and righteousness were beyond reproach.

The king decided to marry the daughter of the fisherman - Satyavati. The greedy fisherman told her daughter to marry the king only if he fulfils two conditions: (1) Devavratha would never aspire for the throne of Hastinapur and (2) He would never marry. These two conditions were too harsh for King Shantanu to accept as it was great injustice towards his beloved son Devavratha.

The king did not accept the conditions and went back to his kingdom with a heavy heart. He remained aloof and took no interest in the matters of the state. Devavratha grew worried for his father and decided to find the root cause of his unhappiness. When he came to know about his father's love for Satyavati and his desire to marry her, Devavratha went to Satyavati and persuaded her to marry his father and become his stepmother.

When Satyavati repeated her two conditions, Devavratha took the oath ("bhishma pratigya") of lifelong celibacy and earned the rightful title of Bhishma – a great warrior. He assured the fisher-woman that he would never marry and only her son would be accepted as the future king of Hastinapur. Happy days returned as King Shantanu married Satyavati. The queen gave birth to two sons who were named as Chitrangada and Vichitravirya.

CHAPTER 2
The Kingdom of Hastinapur

Days passed by and King Shantanu died a natural death due to old age. His elder son Chitrangada also died in young age. Hastinapur came under the rule of Vichitravirya and continued to flourish under his rule. Vichitravirya was married to two princesses, but as fate had it, he could not become a father. Soon, Vichitravirya was also killed in a battle, without any heir. His queens were offered a child each from a great sage, as a blessing through his 'Yogic Power.' The two queens followed the instructions and gave birth to Dhritrashtra and Pandu respectively, but the third time sent their maid to the sage and Vidura was born of the maid as the third son.

Dhritrashtra was blind from birth and therefore, Pandu succeeded the throne of Hastinapur. Pandu, Dhritrashtra and Vidura grew up as friends and conducted the affairs of the state with great foresight. Vidura was most righteous of all and was chosen as the Prime Minister of Hastinapur. Pandu married Kunti (aunt of Sri Krishna) who gave him three sons, Yudhishthira (who was really the son of the

God Dharma), Bhima (who was really the son of the God of Wind, Vayu) and Arjuna (who was really the son of the King of the gods, Indra). He also married Madri, who gave him twin sons, Nakul and Sahadeva (sons of the twin Gods, Ashvins).

Dhritrashtra married Gandhari and she gave birth to Duryodhana, Dushasana and 98 other sons and one daughter, Dushala. Pandu died and Dhritrashtra became the king.

On other hand, having given his word of honour to his stepmother, Satyavati, Bhishma remained celibate all through his life. Marriage was never thought of, nor did any sensual desire ever arise in his mind. This great "Yogi" was adept in many "Yogas" and practice of meditation.

His truthfulness was such that whatever he spoke came true. He knew every martial art and war trick. He was the most respected person in the kingdom of Hastinapur. Reverentially, he was called 'Bhishma Pitamaha'- Grandsire Bhishma.

He served his stepmother, then her son Vichitravirya, later his sons Pandu and Dhritrashtra, as a mark of loyalty to the throne of Hastinapur. He was well aware of the weaknesses and ethical decline in the character of his grandsons and could foresee the cumulative tragedy that was sure to befall the kingdom of Hastinapur. He never made any attempt to become the king of Hastinapur or to dislodge the weak and morally selfish successors to the throne. Vidura, as his best friend, understood the peculiar predicament and mental state of Bhishma.

CHAPTER 3
Story of Arjuna

The princes - Pandu's and Dhritrashtra's sons - grew into wonderful children. After the thread ceremony, they all went for studies to the ashram of their Guru- 'Acharya Drona' (also called Dronacharya) - teacher of the royal family.

Out of all Pandavas and Kauravas, Arjuna had immense liking for the sport of bow and arrow. He practiced this art with great concentration and perseverance. Soon, he became the best student in this art. Acharya Drona was very much pleased with Arjuna and showed preferential love and favour to him. This caused a natural adolescence jealousy in the heart of Duryodhana and his brother Dushasana. Duryodhana, in particular, did not like Arjuna and other Pandavas and silently, ill feelings like hatred towards the Pandavas took birth in his heart. One day, the Kauravas openly criticised their Guru for the favour he showed to Arjuna, telling him that they were not less skilful in archery either. As a reply to their criticism, Acharya Drona arranged a test to decide who was the best archer amongst all of them.

Accordingly, a wooden bird was put on a branch of a distant tree. It was partly hidden by the foliage. A prominent artificial eye was painted on the wooden bird. The teacher called all his disciples and said, "Look my children, a bird is sitting on that far off tree. You have to hit the arrow exactly at its eye. Are you ready?"

Everyone nodded. One by one, they were invited to try their skill. They stretched their bow string and Dronacharya asked them a question, "May I know what is visible to you at this point of time?" Everyone replied innocently, "Why, O Gurudev, I am seeing you, the tree, people around me and the bird!" Acharya told them to step aside, as it was obvious that with such a poor concentration they were sure to miss their target!

Lastly, it was the turn of Arjuna. He readied himself, his bow and arrow in perfect graceful harmony! When the Guru asked him, "O Arjuna, will you tell me what is being observed by you?"

Arjuna replied, "Sir, at this point of time, only the eye of the bird is visible to me." When asked by the teacher whether he was able to see the bird, the tree and the people around him, Arjuna replied in negative, maintaining that he saw the eye of the bird only.

Dronacharya was pleased with Arjuna's immense concentration and correct approach towards the art of

archery. Everyone saw the point, including Duryodhana, but the seed of jealousy was sown in his heart.

All the princes returned to Hastinapur after completing their studies at Drona's ashram. They grew into healthy and powerful adults. All were trained in various branches of knowledge, including statesmanship, diplomacy, economics and sociology. Moreover, everyone excelled in one particular skill of war-game. Yudhishthira was expert in swordsmanship and throwing javelin, while Bhima and Duryodhana excelled in fighting with mace - heavy metal club. Arjuna was excellent in archery. Nakul loved animals and became an excellent trainer while Sahadeva had a great knowledge of astrology.

CHAPTER 4
Story of Eklavya

Near the ashram of Dronacharya, where Arjuna and his brothers took lessons in various arts, there lived a small bright boy who belonged to the tribe of the Nishada. His name was Eklavya. He had a great desire to learn the art of archery from Dronacharya. His father knew that Guru

Drona was the teacher of the royal family and would not accept Eklavya as his disciple. It was futile to dream of such a privilege.

But the boy's determination knew no bounds. When Dronacharya refused to teach him, he found another means to learn. Near his house, under a tree, Eklavya installed a clay idol of Dronacharya that he worshiped as his Guru! The talented young Eklavya soon acquired high knowledge in archery. He attributed his success to his Guru, Dronacharya.

One day, as it happened, Dronacharya and Arjuna were passing by the hut of Eklavya. It was a pleasant and peaceful afternoon and people were taking rest. But constant barking of a dog broke the tranquillity and silence. Eklavya did not like this and therefore, he shut the mouth of the dog with seven arrows without injuring it! Dronacharya and Arjuna were surprised to see the dog with his mouth sealed in such a manner!

Dronacharya was amazed and knew that the archer must be an exceptionally skilled artist. They decided to trace this skilful fellow and reached the spot where Eklavya was practicing wonders with his bow and arrow, in front of the clay image of Drona. It took no time for Dronacharya to understand the situation. He realised that Eklavya was superior to Arjuna in the skill of archery. Dronacharya loved Arjuna and had declared him as the best archer on the earth.

Hence, the Guru thought for a while and came to a decision to remove Eklavya as a competitor to Arjuna.

Dronacharya went to Eklavya and said, "O young man, who has taught you such wonderful skills in archery! Who is your Guru?"

Seeing the Guru in front of him, the boy Eklavya was overjoyed and said, "Why, O Gurudev, this all is your grace! I worship you as my Guru. Look, you are there in that image!"

Dronacharya was pleased with the dedication of Eklavya and said, "I bless you my son. But as is customary, won't you give me my fees – 'Guru-dakshina'!"

Eklavya was overwhelmed to see that Dronacharya had accepted him as his disciple! He said, "O honourable teacher, whatever you ask, this humble disciple of yours will try his utmost to offer you as Guru-dakshina!

Guru Drona said, "Eklavya, I am pleased with your respect for me. I want the thumb of your right hand as my Guru-dakshina." To ask for the thumb of an archer was almost equivalent to kill him! How could Dronacharya demand such a heavy prize from one disciple to protect the honour of the other!

But, Eklavya had no such remorse. Unruffled and with due humility, cheerfully and without protest, he cut his right thumb and placed it at the feet of Dronacharya. Gods in the heaven silently praised the greatness of Eklavya's sacrifice. His loyalty and dedication towards his Guru is praised by people even today!

CHAPTER 5
Karna

Before her marriage, Kunti was immersed in God-worship, meditation and yoga. She undertook arduous austere practices to please the Gods. One day, the sage Durvasa visited Kuntibhoja, the kingdom of Kunti's father. He was extremely pleased with Kunti's efforts in order to make his stay comfortable. He blessed her with a mantra that would enable her to acquire sons from the Gods whom she invoked.

To test her newly acquired power, Kunti(still unmarried) decided to have a son from the Sun God. She prayed and wished for a son as told to her by Durvasa Rishi. And to her astonishment, the most beautiful and powerful son was born to her. Kunti was afraid to face the society for bearing a child before marriage and decided to desert the child who was named Karna. She put the child in a basket and left the basket afloat in the river. A childless couple found the child and was immensely pleased. Karna, powerful and radiant as his father, the Sun God, protected by the armour of 'kavacha' and 'kundalas', grew into an

adolescent boy. Karna's foster parents were charioteers by caste: Adhiratha and Radha by name. Due to his lower caste parentage, Karna is also known as 'Sut-Putra'.

The great Karna, away from Hastinapur, grew up as a very powerful and generous adult. For his studies, Karna went to the ashram of Parashurama, the Guru of Brahmins. Parashurama had decided to take only Brahmin boys as his disciples. Therefore, Karna went there in disguise of a Brahmin boy and learnt old scriptures, Vedas, Upanishads and became exceedingly expert in the art of archery.

One day, sage Parashurama was resting with his head in the lap of Karna. Soon, he fell asleep. Meanwhile, a big insect started biting the thigh of Karna. He felt agonising pain and blood started oozing from the wound. But, he endured the pain lest the sound sleep of his revered Guru would be disturbed. But, the stream of hot blood reached the Guru due to which he was awakened from his sleep. He was amazed at the degree of tolerance and endurance of Karna who did not even stir or move his body. A thought crossed Parashurama's mind: How could a Brahmin boy tolerate such great pain! Only the warrior caste (Kshatriya) is known for such a feat. Parashurama then asked Karna his real name and identity.

Karna could not tell a lie now. He told his story to his Guru and begged his pardon to have come in the disguise of a Brahmin. Parashurama was extremely angry that he was deceived to accept a low caste fellow as his disciple. He cursed Karna that during the most important battle of

his life when he would need his skills most desperately, all his skills would fail him.

The disappointed Karna returned to his parents. His restless heart wanted some change and therefore, he requested his parents to permit him to visit Hastinapur, where he met Duryodhana, his closest mate.

CHAPTER 6
Envious Duryodhana

Bhishma, Dronacharya and Vidura called a meeting to designate the next king, in place of Dhritrashtra. Two options were discussed. First, Yudhishthira being the eldest of the Kuru princes was considered. Second view, supported by Dhritrashtra and his brother-in-law Shakuni (brother of his wife, queen Gandhari and maternal uncle of Duryodhana), was to select Duryodhana as the future king. But the opinion of Bhishma, Dronacharya, Kripacharya (Guru of the Royal House) and Vidura, of nominating Yudhishthira as the heir, apparently prevailed. This naturally caused huge disappointment in Duryodhana's camp. Soon, an opportunity came to the evil-minded Duryodhana and Shakuni to put an end to the Pandavas.

In a nearby town of Varnavata, a grand exhibition was arranged every year. The organisers always sent an invitation to the King of Hastinapur to send some members of the royal family to grace the occasion. This time, Duryodhana and Shakuni persuaded Dhritrashtra to send Pandavas to Varnavata. The king agreed and accordingly the Pandavas were informed. Yudhishthira and his brothers were also happy as they would get the opportunity to mix with the people of their kingdom and get first hand information about their problems and wellbeing. Accompanied by their mother, Kunti, Pandavas decided to attend the exhibition at Varnavata. As was customary, the organisers decided to build a temporary palatial house for their stay. The job was entrusted to one

expert contractor whom Shakuni knew very well. Bribing the fellow, Duryodhana and Shakuni deliberated a secret plan to put an end to the life of Pandavas. It was decided that the palace that would house the Pandavas should be constructed out of highly inflammable material like lac, resins, hemp, oil, fat, etc. The contractor completed his job meticulously and it was not possible to detect any foul play from cursory outward examination of the house.

Duryodhana and Uncle Shakuni arranged to send their secret agent in the guise of a servant, who was instructed to put the house on fire when Pandavas would be fast asleep. Death due to burns would appear as an accident.

Thus, the plan was sure to succeed had the spies of Vidura, the Prime Minister of Hastinapur and the well-wisher of Pandavas, not told Vidura about the same. Vidura, on his part, alerted the Pandavas about the death trap and a solution was offered in the form of digging an underground tunnel in advance, to fool the Kauravas. The tunnel opened in a far off forest.

The house was torched as planned and it burnt to ashes within no time. Pandavas had already left through the tunnel, but five workers and servants were charred to death. Everyone, including Karna, took Pandavas to be dead.

The narrow escape put Kunti in a state of shock and apprehension. She could not put her sons at the mercy of Duryodhana and Shakuni. She was afraid they would again make an attempt on their lives. Therefore, she pleaded her sons to live incognito for the time being. Accordingly, they stayed in the forest for some days.

CHAPTER 7
Pandavas Stay in the Forest

The forest where they escaped was under the rule of the demon Hidimba and his sister Hidimbi. When the demons smelled the flesh of humans, Hidimba decided to kill them and eat them as his food. He sent his sister to assess the situation.

But as fate had it, Hidimbi fell in love with the huge and powerful Bhima. She transformed herself into a beautiful woman and approached Bhima with the desire to marry him. She told the evil designs of her brother to

kill them. Bhima was not afraid and decided to fight it out with Hidimba.

He went with her all alone and challenged the demon chieftain. The ensuing fight was terrible. Both of them fought with great fervour and in the end, Hidimba was killed and Bhima was victorious.

Kunti was very proud of her son Bhima. But the presence of an unknown but beautiful lady by his side puzzled her. Hidimbi then told everyone about her real identity and her desire to marry Bhima. Kunti realised that not only was Hidimbi in true love with her son, but she was also instrumental in saving their lives. Therefore, she allowed Bhima to fulfil the desire of Hidimbi. Bhima agreed on one condition that he would leave her after a son would be born to them. Hidimbi agreed and they were married.

They were blessed with the most powerful and obedient son- Ghatotkacha. This son of Bhima stayed with his mother and promised his father that he would come to his aid whenever he would be called upon.

CHAPTER 8
Marriage of Pandavas

After some time, Kunti and the Pandavas decided to leave the forest and go to a nearby city. Accordingly, disguised as a Brahmin family, they decided to stay in the city of Ekchakra, begging for food from door to door. It was decided that they would equally share whatever they get, amongst themselves.

The days passed by and one day, they came to know about the swayamvar of the beautiful princess of Panchal- Draupadi. Being a princess of the Panchal kingdom, Draupadi was also referred to as 'Panchali.' Arjuna knew about the bravery and beauty of Draupadi and in fact was desirous of marrying her.

Sri Krishna, King of Dwaraka, had meanwhile become a friend and saviour of the Pandavas. Arjuna respected Sri Krishna as his chosen ideal and guide. On the other hand, princess Draupadi had accepted Sri Krishna as her brother and guide. Therefore, Sri Krishna was interested in the marriage of Draupadi with Arjuna.

Draupadi was a very brave and beautiful woman. She was equally intelligent. She had put a condition for her marriage that she would wed the prince who would pierce the eye of the rotating wooden fish by looking at its reflection. The competing prince had to look at this reflection and hit the eye of the fish above, with an arrow. Only one chance would be given to each prince.

Many princes from all over India had come to try their luck in getting her as their bride. Duryodhana, Karna, Arjuna (in the disguise of a Brahmin) and other Pandavas were a few amongst them. Draupadi was waiting for Arjuna to succeed. Sri Krishna, who was present as an observer, felt likewise.

Soon the competition began. One after another, great archers tried their skills, but in vain. Then arose Karna, the expert. Saluting the king and others present in the court, he approached to undertake the difficult but possible test that would give him Draupadi as his bride.

Draupadi got up and raised an objection saying, "O noble one, who are your parents? As far as I know, you are a lowly sut-putra and I have no desire to marry you. You do not qualify to take this test." The insult made Karna red with anger, but he could do nothing. What Draupadi had said was true and everyone in the hall agreed. The duo of Duryodhana and Karna left the court of King Drupad, father of Draupadi, and vowed to avenge the insult at some time in the future.

Next, it was the turn of Arjuna to try his skills and win over the hand of his prospective bride. He saluted Sri Krishna and pierced the eye of the fish in one go. Draupadi was immensely pleased and put the garland in the neck of Arjuna. Thus, they were married.

As soon as they reached their small hut, the Pandavas announced their arrival and told their mother Kunti to guess what they had brought that day. Kunti replied innocently– "Divide the gift amongst yourselves and enjoy." This terrible command now applied to Draupadi. Thus, Draupadi became the wife of all the five brothers.

Meanwhile, Arjuna visited many places of pilgrimage and reached the kingdom of Dwaraka, which was ruled by

Sri Krishna. The elder brother of Sri Krishna, Balarama, had decided to give the hand of their sister Subhadra to Duryodhana in marriage. Sri Krishna did not approve of this marriage and wanted Subhadra to wed Arjuna. Therefore, he asked Arjuna to secretly run away with his sister and marry her. They eloped and got married. Later on, they had a brave son named Abhimanyu.

CHAPTER 9
Indraprastha

After their marriage, the Pandavas revealed to the Kuru clan that they were still alive. They were invited back to Hastinapur. Sri Krishna, Bhishma, Dronacharya and others persuaded Dhritrashtra to give them their rightful half of the kingdom with due honour. Dhritrashtra acceded to their wishes, though somewhat reluctantly. Duryodhana and Uncle Shakuni opposed the idea and Karna maintained that war would be a better recourse to settle the issue. But, better sense prevailed and according to the dictate of King Dhritrashtra, part of the kingdom was given to Yudhishthira and his brothers.

Khandavavana, a sparsely populated area with meagre facilities for trade and agriculture came to Pandavas lot. However, they did not grumble and took a developed Indraprastha as their capital city. All five brothers worked hard to bring prosperity to Indraprastha. People joined their labour and soon Indraprastha became as glorious as Hastinapur.

Saints and sages, Gods and angels, all preferred Indraprastha to Hastinapur for touring and pilgrimage. Even plant and animal life prospered due to the righteous behaviour of Pandavas. Gods in the heaven showered continuous blessings on them. Thus, over a period of many years, gradually but surely, Pandavas were recognised and accepted as powerful, noble and better rulers than Kauravas. Sri Krishna visited them off and on and Arjuna became his friend and best disciple.

On the other hand, the development of Khandavavana infuriated Duryodhana and his uncle Shakuni. They were not happy with the glorious progress and prosperity of their cousins at Indraprastha. Jealousy and hatred, as is well known, create conditions for revenge and meanness. Duryodhana and Shakuni wanted to put an end to the well being of the Pandavas either by hook or by crook.

They started to analyse the strengths and weaknesses of their counterparts. Duryodhana knew that it was futile to attack them or engage the Pandavas in war, as it would surely lead to the downfall of Hastinapur. It was also sensed that Sri Krishna, Bhishma and Dronacharya would oppose any such move.

At last, Uncle Shakuni, the great schemer, found the weak point that he was looking for. He knew that Yudhishthira as a king would not refuse to play a game of dice if a royal invitation was sent to him.

Shakuni was adept in this game of dice. He had specially prepared the dice that followed his command. He could very easily fix the game and the victory of the Kauravas was assured. Thus, after proper persuasion, Dhritrashtra sent an invitation to Yudhishthira to participate in the game of dice.

At Indraprastha, Kunti protested and warned them not to engage in this gambling game as it might lead to disaster. But the determined Yudhishthira could not disregard his duty as a king and decided to accept the invitation.

Accordingly, the five brothers and their wife Draupadi reached Hastinapur. A warm welcome awaited them. Pandavas saluted Bhishma, Dronacharya and Vidura and sought their blessings. The elders were well wishers of the Pandavas and cautioned Yudhishthira to be careful of the ill designs of Shakuni and Duryodhana. But destiny had a more important role to play in their lives.

CHAPTER 10
Game of Dice

The day for the game of dice was fixed. On one side sat Duryodhana, Uncle Shakuni and Dushasana while Yudhishthira and his four brothers occupied the other side. Karna was also a part of the assembly. Shakuni would throw the dice for Kauravas while Yudhishthira would do the job for Pandavas.

Initially, a small amount of money and jewellery was put at stake. The dice was rolled and Shakuni won the throw. Thus, the game progressed on and on, every time Shakuni came up with the requisite number with his magical dice.

But, as a losing gambler, Yudhishthira lost reason and discrimination. He put Indraprastha at stake and lost that turn too. Mocking him further, uncle Shakuni challenged Yudhishthira that he had nothing left to put at stake now. The insulting words, instead of dissuading him, further stimulated him to play and regain the lost kingdom. Hope never dies for a gambler! Yudhishthira asked Shakuni to continue the game. He put his brothers at stake. As a result,

Bhima became the servant of Duryodhana. On similar lines, Yudhishthira lost Arjuna, Nakul, Sahadeva and at last himself to the evil designs of Shakuni. Pandavas were bereft of all rights, even those of ordinary citizens!

At last, the desperate gambler in Yudhishthira put Draupadi at stake! Everyone, almost everyone in the court protested, but in vain. Draupadi became the serving maid of Duryodhana and Kauravas. Victorious

and lustful Duryodhana asked his brother Dushasana to bring Draupadi to the court. He obeyed his elder brother and brought the helpless Draupadi dragging her by the hair. Her protest that Yudhishthira had no right to put her at stake was not heard in the agonising cries of the ladies in the court. Heads drooped with shame. Bhishma, Dronacharya and Vidura could do nothing. King Dhritrashtra was silent.

Duryodhana ordered Dushasana to disrobe the lady. Bhishma objected, Dhritrashtra trembled, but the lust, pride and blind power of victory was not prepared to listen or see sense. The mighty Karna, who was the best friend of Duryodhana, got an opportunity to avenge the insult he had faced at Draupadi's swayamvar and thus, he questioned the chastity of Draupadi by commenting that a woman with five husbands can never be a decent woman.

Helpless Draupadi had but one hope, one last hope to save her grace. Sri Krishna could alone save her from disgrace! She prayed to Sri Krishna and he provided unending lengths of cloth on the body of Draupadi.

Here, Dushasana pulled one yard of her sari and their two yards were added by the kind Sri Krishna. At last, Dushasana collapsed, completely exhausted. But still, Shakuni and Duryodhana were not to be put off. Duryodhana, baring his thigh, invited Draupadi to sit on it. The infuriated Bhima rose to kill Duryodhana but was prevented by Yudhishthira to act.

And then Bhima vowed, "Listen everyone, listen O Dhritrashtra, I will kill Duryodhana by breaking open his thigh and would drink blood from the same. And moreover, O evil Dushasana, remember and tremble in the heart, for I will break open your chest and colour the hair of Draupadi with that blood."

CHAPTER 11
Second Game of Dice

The scene in the royal court was of immense anger, frustration and grief. All these emotions combined together to take the form of protest against Shakuni and Duryodhana. Bhishma, Dronacharya and Vidura all objected to this shameless humiliation of a lady of their own family, that too the queen! They rebuked Duryodhana for his actions and warned him to act with some restraint and ethics. They objected to the fixing of the dice game and appealed to Dhritrashtra to restore *status quo ante*.

Dhritrashtra accepted their plea and declared the results of the dice game as null and void. He was also not in agreement with the obnoxious behaviour of his son and brother-in-law. The kingdom of Indraprastha was duly returned and Yudhishthira and his brothers and wife Draupadi were declared free from the bondage.

Shakuni continued to plan for the final kill. He persuaded Duryodhana and Dhritrashtra to invite Yudhishthira again for the last and final game of dice. Shakuni knew the mentality of a gambler king. He was sure that Yudhishthira would still have to play the game if royal invitation is sent and proper conditions were laid. Next day, as Yudhishthira and his brothers were about to leave for Indraprastha, Uncle Shakuni invited Yudhishthira for the final game on behalf of Duryodhana and consented by Dhritrashtra. He himself put the condition for the game as, "O Yudhishthira, in this game, whosoever loses will

relinquish his kingdom and go to forest exile for twelve years, with an additional one year of incognito living. If detected in the last year, again an exile of twelve years will ensue." Yudhishthira agreed and lost the final game as well.

As a result, all the five Pandavas and Draupadi put on simple robes and left for the forest. Their mother Kunti, being weak and old, stayed back with Vidura.

CHAPTER 12
Life in Exile

The Pandavas started their exile and reached Kamyak Forest and decided to rest there for a while. The news of their exile reached Sri Krishna, the ruler of Dwaraka. He was related to Pandavas as a cousin brother and was their friend, saviour and guide.

Sri Krishna reached Kamyak forest to meet the Pandavas and Draupadi. After inquiring about their well being, he advised Pandavas to be vigilant and not lose heart. He explained to them that suffering and sorrows bring the requisite feeling of renunciation essential to seek higher goal in life.

But the recent insult at the hands of Duryodhana, Dushasana and Karna was fresh in the mind of Draupadi. She had not even forgotten the scornful laughter of Duryodhana and Shakuni. All these memories made Draupadi emotional and angry. Speaking out her heart to the Lord, she said in anguish:

"O Krishna, how is it that this Draupadi, sister of the Lord of the Universe and wife of five brave, powerful and invincible Pandavas, has to go through such horrible time? Was it not their duty to protect me and punish the miscreants? Was that fair on the part of Dhritrashtra to allow Dushasana to drag me by my hair and attempt to remove my only clothing? Does Yudhishthira has the right to put me at stake when he himself had become slave of Duryodhana? And even if the husband becomes a slave, does he lose the right to come to the rescue of his wife, does he lose the right to protect the honour of his wife?"

The barrage of questions affected Sri Krishna intensely. With due seriousness, he proclaimed, "O dear sister, do not grieve. I promise you that every woman of the Kaurava clan will shed more tears than what you have shed, for the non-righteous Kauravas and their supporters in this shameful act are sure to perish at the hands of the Pandavas very soon."

Sri Krishna told one more interesting thing to her. He said that if he had been there in the court of Dhritrashtra during the game of dice, he would not have allowed the game to be played in the first place. He would have impressed upon everyone, including Bhishma and Dhritrashtra, how gambling leads to total corruption and degeneration of the race. He would have forcefully prohibited Duryodhana from engaging in such vice. Gambling, smoking, drinking, hunting and prostitution are the curse on human beings and every righteous person should labour to avoid these vices. The persons who engage in these acts are doomed to destruction and moral death. They suffer for their ill-deeds and are destined to defeat in every endeavour.

CHAPTER 13
Story of Sage Durvasa

The question of daily food for the Pandavas and their wife was solved by the gift given to Draupadi by the Sun God- a special vessel that would be filled by the desired food once a day. However, once it was used in a day, it would get refilled only the next day.

One day, sage Durvasa and his disciples were passing through the forest. They reached the hut of the Pandavas. Sage Durvasa was known for his short temper and would invoke a curse on anyone who did not obey his commands.

Draupadi welcomed the sage and after proper salutations, inquired about their needs. Durvasa told her that they all were hungry and would be happy to receive proper meals. Draupadi was at her wits' end, as there was nothing in her kitchen to offer to these hundred pious guests! Unfortunately, the vessel that could have solved her problem was already used for the day and washed clean. Now, it would yield the food only on the next day. But it was absolutely essential for her to make some

arrangements as per the command of Durvasa, lest his curse might prove disastrous for her and the Pandavas.

To buy some time, she requested the sage and his disciples to take a bath in the nearby river and in the meantime, she would prepare the meals for them. The sage agreed and left for the river with his associates.

Perturbed and helpless, Draupadi started praying to Sri Krishna for help. She sat in front of the image of the Lord and with wet eyes prayed to Him to rush to her assistance. Sri Krishna, in his palace in Dwaraka, heard the cry of despair of his devotee and rushed to her forest dwelling. With a sweet musical voice, he consoled her not to worry and asked her for some food for himself. He said that he was hungry.

Draupadi was unable to comprehend this unusual demand. She had told Sri Krishna that she was facing a shortage of food and needed help. But Sri Krishna himself appeared to trouble her. This paradox confused her. Then he asked her to bring the vessel that gave her the daily food.

Reluctantly, Draupadi did as she was told. She brought the vessel to him and there, attached to the back of the vessel, was a grain of rice! Sri Krishna put it in his mouth. His hunger was satisfied. And then occurred a miracle. The Lord of the Universe had eaten enough and with this the appetite of the whole world was satisfied!

On the bank of the river, Durvasa and his disciples suddenly felt their stomachs were full! They had no appetite left even for a single morsel of food. How could they now eat the meals prepared by Draupadi? Therefore, the sage with his party hastily retreated, without bothering Draupadi anymore.

CHAPTER 14
Skilful Arjuna

To increase their power and capabilities, the Pandavas decided to send Arjuna to the kingdom of Himalayas and the heaven, to bring special divine missiles from the Gods. Moreover, Arjuna would be able to learn a few more skills from them.

On one auspicious day, Arjuna left for his mission. His first destination was Mount Kailash, in the heights of Himalayas, abode of Lord Shiva. One day, he encountered a beautiful deer freely jumping here and there. He shot an arrow at the deer to hunt it down. At the same time, another arrow from the opposite direction hit the deer. Arjuna saw a local tribesman opposite him, with a bow and arrow in his hand. The deer lay dead with two arrows in his chest. It was undecided as to whose arrow had killed the deer. It was essential to establish one's right over the kill. Both Arjuna and the tribesman staked their claim.

A bitter fight ensued. After their arrows were exhausted, they were engaged in wrestling. The apparently weak tribesman brought Arjuna to his wits' end. No one was willing to relent. Arjuna was surprised to find his inability to defeat even a simple tribesman. He, therefore, requested the tribesman to reveal his true identity. Arjuna said, "O brave fighter, you must not be what you appear, for it is impossible for anyone to compete with me in the game of archery."

And yes indeed, the tribesman was none other than Lord Shiva himself! Pleased with Arjuna, Shiva appeared

before him in his Divine form and as an act of blessing, gave Arjuna his most powerful divine missile.

From there Arjuna went to Indralok, the kingdom of Indra(Heaven) through the beautiful provinces of Moon, Stars and Planets. In fact, the king of Gods, Lord Indra was his father, as Kunti had obtained Arjuna from Indra through her yogic powers.

Besides archery and other martial arts, here Arjuna learnt music and dance from Urvashi, the most beautiful celestial nymph. She fell in love with Arjuna, but Arjuna had no such feelings towards her since she was his teacher. Thus, disappointed in love, Urvashi invoked a curse on Arjuna that he would become a eunuch for one year. This curse later proved to be beneficial for him and helped him during his exile to stay incognito for one year.

CHAPTER 15
Disguise

The twelve year period of the exile finally came to an end. Pandavas decided to pass the last (thirteenth) year incognito, as decreed, in the capital city of King Virata. In order to avoid detection, the Pandavas along with their wife disguised themselves as follows:

Yudhishthira— As he was well versed with both the scriptures and skills of dice, rules and functioning of the royal court, Yudhishthira decided to serve the king, in the capacity of his adviser and priest. He assumed the name Kanka.

Bhima- His mighty and huge body required much food to satisfy his appetite. Therefore, Bhima decided to work in the royal kitchen as the chief cook assuming the name of Ballava.

Arjuna- Arjuna was destined to pass one year as a eunuch (thanks to the curse of Urvashi). Therefore, it was decided that he would teach dance and music to the princess Uttara, in the guise of a eunuch, assuming the name Brihannala.

Nakul- He was an expert in the training and treatment of horses. So he became Granthika, the caretaker and guard of the horse stable.

Sahadeva- Sahadeva knew about tending the cattle and milking the cows. So he became the in charge of cow sheds and called himself Tantipala.

Draupadi- She was a specialist in designing the hair in different styles and thus, she was appointed as the maid

servant to the queen. She was to be known as Sairandhri.

Thus, separately, without letting other people know that they were related, all the Pandavas and Draupadi entered into the service of King Virata, in the hope that the agents of Kauravas would not be able to spot them and inform Duryodhana about their hide out in the incognito year.

CHAPTER 16
Story of Keechaka

Keechaka was the brother-in-law of King Virata and he was also the commander of the King's army. Keechaka was a powerful and lustful man. He was attracted towards the beauty and youthfulness of Draupadi (Sairandhri), the maid servant of his sister.

He started making passes at her and instructed his attendants to tell her to bring food and drinks to his room.

Draupadi was aware of his evil nature. Secretly, she told the powerful Bhima about Keechaka and his dirty overtures. The angry Bhima told her to accept Keechaka's invitation to go to his room that night. Keechaka was blinded with lust and drinks. He waited for Draupadi to come to his room. But instead of her, Bhima went with the glass of milk for Keechaka, dressed in a lady's attire.

The ensuing fight between Bhima and Keechaka was very intense as both were equally powerful. Bhima in the end prevailed and Keechaka was killed.

King Virata came to know about the sad end to his

ignoble brother-in-law. He was particularly displeased with him because he tried to take undue advantage of a maid. Death of such a disgraceful person, in fact, did not hurt the king in any way. He kept the matter to himself by announcing that Keechaka would be away from the capital for a few months. In fact, King Virata fought on the side of the Pandavas in the war.

CHAPTER 17
War Clouds Loom Large

The Pandavas successfully fulfilled all the conditions of banishment and ended their exile. Duryodhana and Shakuni were now left with no option but to offer Pandavas their due portion of the kingdom. To part with a part of land and wealth was not acceptable to Duryodhana. Therefore, when Sri Krishna came to them as an envoy of the Pandavas to ask for their share of land, Duryodhana downrightly refused to give anything to the Pandavas.

The Kauravas were hundred in numbers and not at all afraid of the five Pandavas. Moreover, there was no army to support the Pandavas in the upcoming war. Kauravas were sure to win even if Arjuna and Bhima convinced Yudhishthira to indulge in a war. Accordingly, Arjuna was sent to Dwaraka to seek advice and help from Sri Krishna.

When Arjuna reached Dwaraka, he was surprised to find that Duryodhana had also come there to seek help from Sri Krishna. His main purpose was to ask for Sri Krishna's army to fight on his side. Sri Krishna was asleep when they went to meet him and were asked to wait for some time. Duryodhana took his seat beside the head of the Lord, while Arjuna sat by his holy feet. In a while, Sri Krishna opened his eyes to see his dear friend and disciple at his feet. Said the lord, "O Arjuna, what brings you here so early in the morning?"

But Duryodhana could not wait; he intervened and said, "O Krishna, I have come before Arjuna. Therefore, please speak to me first."

The Lord jested, "But I saw Arjuna first. Let him talk to me first."

But, the sober Arjuna himself told the Lord, "No, Duryodhana is right. He has come before me. Let him put forward his purpose of visit."

Thus, given the chance, Duryodhana asked Sri Krishna to fight on his side. Sri Krishna said, "But Duryodhana, I have vowed not to pick up arms in this war. But my army can be on your side. Decide what you want, me or my army."

The foolish Duryodhana thought: "There is no use of Sri Krishna if he is not fighting, I will ask for his huge army." Thus, the army of Sri Krishna went to the side of Kauravas. Arjuna was pleased, for all that the Pandavas wanted was the gracious Lord on their side. He thanked Duryodhana for his choice.

The inevitability of war left both the Kauravas and the Pandavas to chalk out their respective strategies and assess the strength and weaknesses of their opponents. While Arjuna was the best archer on the Pandavas side, Karna was no less a warrior on the Kauravas side. Someone had even rated him as greater than Arjuna. This particular fact caused a great concern for their mother Kunti.

CHAPTER 18
War of Kurukshetra

The war was to be fought in accordance with a certain set of rules. Various rules and regulations were laid down for this Dharma Yuddha, the war of righteousness. Some of these ethical rules were:

- The war would be fought from dawn to dusk.
- No more than one warrior would attack a single warrior.
- Injured and helpless soldiers who had lost their weapon would not be attacked.
- Fight would be between equals, a charioteer would engage the other charioteer only and not a pedestrian soldier.
- No one should attack anyone from behind.
- The rules pertaining to a specific weapon would be followed. For instance, striking below the waist in mace warfare would be considered unfair.

The war started on a highly moralistic note but later both the sides took to dishonourable and unethical acts to gain victory. It lasted for 18 days.

The whole scenario of the battlefield of Kurukshetra and the description of each and every event that happened in these 18 days was narrated to Dhritrashtra by his charioteer and advisor Sanjaya, who had been gifted with the divine vision by the sage Vyasa.

On the side of the Kauravas, Bhishma led the front. Besides him, Dronacharya, Duryodhana, Jayadratha and many more warriors were fighting against the Pandavas. Karna would be out of the picture till Bhishma was alive and leading the Kauravas. On the Pandavas side, Sri Krishna became the charioteer of Arjuna. Besides the five brothers, their five sons from Draupadi, King Virata, Abhimanyu- son of Arjuna from Subhadra, Ghatotkacha- son of Bhima from Hidimbi, brother of Draupadi and many more joined the forces.

The fateful day finally dawned. Battle lines were drawn. The two sides were arrayed against each other. Conches and trumpets were blown. The horses and chariots were ready and the elephants were decorated. Arrows and javelins were sharpened, clubs and maces flashed with terrifying power. Duryodhana reached near the chariot of Bhishma and told him about the powerful generals on his side. Bhishma appealed to all the warriors to fight to the end.

CHAPTER 19
Krishna Preached Gita

Amidst the massive slaughter at both the sides, there was a brave warrior who found himself suddenly overwhelmed with the feeling of mental depression, grief and fear when he realised that he had to fight with his close relatives- brothers, uncles and teachers– who were now presented as his enemies. Arjuna was greatly disturbed about the

outcome of the war and the destruction and death that was sure to follow. Therefore, he turned to Sri Krishna, his friend, his teacher and told him about his dilemma.

Lord Sri Krishna understood the emotional pangs of Arjuna and tried to provide him solace. He said, "O Brave one, why are you so worried about these things and that too at this hour! Why have you given yourself to unmanliness and cowardice? You cannot neglect your duties and run away from the war. If you do this, you will bring shame and disgrace to your name for the generations to come."

On listening to this rebuke, Arjuna steadied himself. Sri Krishna tried to put some sense into him and made him rise above his dejection and do his duty selflessly. Thus was born the *Bhagavad Gita* that consists of eighteen chapters with a total of 700 verses. It explains the concept of Dharma, the aim of human birth, the acceptance of truth and the realization of the self through the description of the four Yogas– 'jnana yoga', 'bhakti yoga', 'karma yoga' and 'raja yoga.' Sri Krishna exhorted Arjuna to fight the war without thinking about the consequences. The duty of a person as a Karma Yogi is to do the work allotted to him as he worships God, without expecting any definite fruits thereof. Selfless work done with full heart and perfection is the best way for the worldly person to realise his inner self. In fact, efficiency in work itself is Yoga!

In the form of this divine book, Sri Krishna provided eternal knowledge to the mankind to conduct their lives in an ethical and fruitful manner. It is still considered one of the most holy books and could be found in almost everyone's home. It imparts the essential wisdom to the human race and acts as a manual to lead a life that is worth living.

In the end, Arjuna said "My Lord. My ignorance has vanished. I have gained my memory through your Grace."

Finally, Arjuna took the command of his army and arranged his men in a special format, which gave little scope to Kauravas' army to advance and attack the Pandavas. Sons of King Virata, Uttar and Shveta had been killed by Bhishma and Shalya respectively. Pandavas saw great loss of their men. Multitudes of soldiers on both sides were killed.

CHAPTER 20
Downfall of Bhishma

Bhishma arranged his army in eagle's format and the Pandavas opted for semi-lunar style to counter Kauravas offensive. Bhima attacked Duryodhana with an arrow that made him unconscious, but he was quickly shifted to a safer place. Now, the ferocious Bhishma attacked the Pandavas with a force unheard of. Pandavas' army was torn apart at tens and hundreds of places. Soldiers started running here and there. Scores of them died on the battle field, in their futile attempt to attack or escape the mighty Bhishma.

Sri Krishna told Arjuna to protect his men by attacking their leader Bhishma. There was no other way but to remove Bhishma if the Pandavas wished to win the war. Arjuna was faltering; many arrows from Bhishma had hit Arjuna. He was bleeding profusely.

Sri Krishna got angry at Arjuna's incapability to defeat Bhishma and took the wheel of a fallen chariot to finish him off. Seeing the Lord rushing towards him, Bhishma

dropped his weapons. With tears flowing from his eyes, Bhishma spoke thus, "O Keshava, O Merciful, how lucky is it that the Lord of the Universe has decided to liberate this ordinary Bhishma from the snares of worldliness." Sri Krishna was reminded of his vow. He threw away the wheel and retreated back to his chariot.

The immeasurable loss caused to the army of the Pandavas at the hands of Bhishma had made it extremely important to defeat him. It was suggested to bring Shikhandi into picture who was a eunuch. As Bhishma had vowed not to fight a eunuch, it was decided that Arjuna should hit the old man under the cover.

The battle of tenth day began. Shikhandi was in the front attacking Bhishma. Bhishma however, said, "Get away, O Shikhandi, I do not want to fight with you."

Thus, the mighty and powerful Bhishma laid down his arms. Arjuna's arrows penetrated his body and Bhishma fell down. There were so many arrows in his body that when he fell down, it looked like he was lying on a bed of arrows! His head was hanging, which Arjuna supported by placing three arrows under the head and neck. Bhishma had promised his father that he would keep the kingdom of Hastinapur secure till the day he died. He used the boon of "icha-mrityu" that had been given to him by his father and decided not to die until the war was over. He requested Sri Krishna to take him to a far off corner of the battleground and a peaceful shelter was arranged for this grand old Kuru.

Every day, after the day's battle was over, Yudhishthira and his brothers visited Bhishma and took lessons on politics and religion at his holy feet.

CHAPTER 21
Dronacharya Takes Over

After the fall of Bhishma, the mighty Karna was brought into the picture. Now, Dronacharya became the commander of the Kauravas' army. Drona was a great warrior with supreme expertise in the game of war and all the instruments of battle. It was not possible for anyone to defeat him.

Meanwhile, Sri Krishna advised the Pandavas to call Ghatotkacha who would wreck havoc in Kauravas' army and Karna would be forced to use his Special 'Vaasavi Astra' on him, instead of Arjuna.

Accordingly, he was called and was told to fight and annihilate the Kauravas' army. Karna was in search of Arjuna, but Ghatotkacha obstructed his path. Moreover, Ghatotkacha vomited fire and threw large quantity of boulders and sand on Kauravas. There was total chaos in Kauravas' camp. Duryodhana now requested Karna to kill this demon, otherwise nobody would remain alive. Reluctantly, Karna had to use 'his onetime use'

Vaasavi Astra on Ghatotkacha instead of Arjuna. Thus, Ghatotkacha died but saved the life of Arjuna.

But this was not the end; still more lives of the loved ones were to be sacrificed in order to save the Pandavas. The death of many stalwarts had put Duryodhana in a fix. In order to overcome this loss, he had arranged his army in an impregnable wheel format, known as the 'Chakra Formation' or the 'Chakravyuh'. On the side of Pandavas, only Krishna and Arjuna knew how to penetrate it but

they were kept busy by the Samsaptakas on the other side of the battlefield. Abhimanyu, son of Arjuna, was capable of penetrating this format, but he did not know how to come out of it. He had heard his father explain it to his mother when he was still in her womb. But Subhadra had fallen asleep when Arjuna was explaining how to come out of it and therefore, Abhimanyu only had half knowledge about the Chakravyuh. This teenage lad, however, pleaded his uncles to allow him to enter the enemy ranks and then, they all could come to help him inside. Kauravas allowed him to enter but soon sealed off the entry of his uncles. All Kaurava warriors attacked the lone but brave Abhimanyu, who fought gallantly all alone against them.

The others were anxious to reach him but were obstructed by a large force of Kauravas' army. Soon, inside the circle, Abhimanyu lost his bow, his chariot was broken and he was without any weapon to defend him. Without mercy and consideration for the helpless state of Abhimanyu, Jayadratha kicked him with his foot and killed him with his sword.

The news of the brave Abhimanyu's death spread all over. Arjuna was deeply grieved and tears rolled down his eyes. The evening halted the battle for the day. Arjuna vowed to kill Jayadratha by the evening of the next day or else give his body up in the burning flames.

Next day, all the warriors on Kauravas side surrounded Jayadratha's chariot and prevented anyone from approaching him. Jayadratha was almost invisible. In the hours of the approaching dusk, the sky became dark and everyone thought that the sun had set. The sky was dark because of a total eclipse of the sun on that day, at that hour and not because it was evening. As Jayadratha was looking in merriment, the eclipse ended and the sun came out. The sunlight was bright and the sharp penetrating arrow left the bow of Arjuna to take the head of Jayadratha far off in jungle, into the lap of his father. Thus, Arjuna kept his vow and avenged the death of his beloved son.

CHAPTER 22
Story Comes to an End

To defeat Dronacharya, Sri Krishna planned a new gimmick. On the side of Pandavas, there was an elephant by the name Ashwatthama. This was the name of the son of Dronacharya as well. Sri Krishna told Yudhishthira to spread the rumour that Ashwatthama was dead! Everyone

knew that Yudhishthira was a righteous person and he refused to speak anything other than the truth. In effect, the elephant was killed and everyone including Yudhishthira shouted, "Ashwatthama is dead, Ashwatthama is dead!" Dronacharya heard these words and suspected that his only son was killed in the battle. Dronacharya, in the din and bustle, failed to hear the second half of the sentence ("...not the man but the elephant") and thinking that his loving son had died, he gave up the fight and got killed.

After Drona, Karna took over the charge of the Kuru army and soon declared either he would survive or Arjuna. The ferocious battle left more than half the soldiers dead. Pandavas were terrified.

Troubled Kunti went to meet Karna that night. With a heavy heart, she begged and pleaded for Arjuna's life, dissuading Karna from fighting the war. During this encounter, Karna came to know the truth about his birth and how Kunti had deserted him at the mercy of river waters. And that the Sun God was in fact his father.

Kunti was willing to announce him as her son now and offered him the throne of Hastinapur if he decided to fight on the side of his brothers, the Pandavas. But Karna had declared his loyalty to Duryodhana. He politely declined Kunti's offer and said, "O mother, I promise you one thing, in any event, you shall have your five sons alive. If Arjuna dies, I shall be the fifth, otherwise, there would be no change in your life."

Sri Krishna knew that Karna was a better archer than Arjuna and could defeat him quite easily. He sent Indra, the foster father of Arjuna, to rob Karna of his protective kavacha and kundalas given to him by his father, the Sun God. It was a very well known fact that Karna was the most generous person on the earth and that he would not disappoint anyone who begged anything of him. Thus, Indra disguised as a Brahmin beggar, came to Karna and requested him for his kavacha and kundalas. Karna, without any hesitation, tore out the natural protective armour and handed it over to Indra. This rendered Karna essentially weak.

Next day, Arjuna and Karna encountered each other in the battlefield. Arrows after arrows tried to find weakness in each other's skill, but no, both Arjuna and Karna were found to be equals. Now came the crucial factor of that curse of Guru Parashurama. The wheel of Karna's chariot jammed and it tilted to one side. Sri Krishna told Arjuna to take advantage of the situation and kill Karna. But Arjuna refused to attack the enemy in distress. But Sri Krishna reminded Arjuna of the laughter of Karna at the pathetic condition of Draupadi in the royal court. Thus, came the end of a great warrior, the greatest archer of the world and the eldest son of Kunti. The Kauravas were falling down one by one, but Bhima was still not satisfied. He had vowed to kill Dushasana and Duryodhana. To that end, Bhima took permission of Yudhishthira and Sri Krishna and killed Dushasana in a brief fight.

But, with Duryodhana, the mace or club fight went on and on. It was fierce and terrifying. Both Bhima and Duryodhana were well built and adept in the skills of fighting. Moreover, Duryodhana had been given the ultimate protection by his mother. Gandhari had removed the blindfold for the first time in her life after marriage and through her powers she had made his body extremely strong. He was supposed to stand naked before his mother but Sri Krishna asked him to wear at least the loincloth. As a result, the thighs were the only part of Duryodhana's body that were left weak. Sri Krishna indicated Bhima by patting on his thigh, and he hit Duryodhana below the

belt. Duryodhana's thigh was broken and he was left there to die a slow and undignified death.

Thus, the war ended after 18 days of destruction. Except for Sri Krishna, the five Pandavas, Draupadi and a few others, everyone was killed in this Great War of Mahabharata.

After reigning supreme for many years, the five brothers, accompanied by Draupadi, started for Himalayas, renouncing the kingdom and all luxuries. A dog also accompanied Yudhishthira. On the way, everyone died, but the dog remained with Yudhishthira.

Soon, they reached the doors of Heaven. The lord of Heaven, Indra, appeared before Yudhishthira and said: "O noble one, welcome to the kingdom of Heavens. You are most righteous person who ever lived on the earth; therefore, we are pleased to welcome you. But there is one condition. This dog cannot be admitted to this holy place of heavens. You come alone and leave the dog behind."

To this, Yudhishthira objected. On hearing Yudhishthira speak thus, the dog changed himself in the form of Dharma itself and said: "O Yudhishthira, the people in coming generations for time immemorial will praise and remember you as the most righteous person ever born. Come let us enjoy the heavenly bliss."

www.ingramcontent.com/pod-product-compliance
Lightning Source LLC
LaVergne TN
LVHW091317080426
835510LV00007B/525